Amazing British Columbia

Amazing British Columbia

Design and Production: Wendy Crumpler, Maxart.com
Printed in Canada by Friesens, Altona, Manitoba.

Library and Archives Canada Cataloguing in Publication

Owen, Audrey

Amazing British Columbia / Audrey Owen.

ISBN 978-0-9813476-0-8

1. Natural history--British Columbia--Juvenile literature. 2. British Columbia--Juvenile literature. 3. English language--Alphabet--Juvenile literature. 4. Alphabet books. I. Title.

QH48.O94 2009   j508.711   C2009-906584-3

Amazing British Columbia

A Natural History from A to Z

by Audrey Owen

Steppingstone Resources   Gibsons, BC

You can fit Canada's biggest lizard across your dinner plate. But first you'd have to catch it. That's hard. The shy **alligator lizard** usually hides under bark or rocks. There it finds food: insects, spiders, and snails.

If the lizard is attacked, part of its tail breaks off and twitches. The predator pounces on the loose tail. Then the alligator lizard slips away to hide and grow a new tail.

a

This lizard is coming out of his hiding spot to bask in the sun.

B

A **black bear** can be black, brown, cinnamon, or even creamy white. It grows quickly the first year. A black bear is as big as a stick of butter when it is born. The mother's milk is very rich. After eight months the cub weighs about 35 kg (75 pounds). Pretend a human baby grew at the same rate. It would weigh about 450 kg (1000 pounds) before its first birthday!

b

A cinnamon black bear cub is out for a stroll in Manning Park.

C

The dainty orchid, **calypso** (Kal-IP-so), is also called a fairy slipper. It lives in dark, damp, old forests. If you walk too near, you can damage calypso's delicate roots. They grow near the top of soft leaf litter. A calypso takes many years to grow. So if you see one, please leave it where it is.

c

Watch for calypso early in Spring.

D

The wood of **dogwood** trees is very hard. Long ago the first people used it to make spears, bows, and arrows. Later, settlers made piano keys from the same wood.

But it was Mrs. Davis who first called the dogwood our provincial flower. She made green and white dogwood leather lapel pins to sell. The money bought wool for socks. Mrs. Davis sent the socks to World War II soldiers.

Now, people plant beautiful dogwoods in their gardens.

d

Dogwood trees bloom on this Vancouver street. Later, red fruit appears. Then the leaves turn colour and fall. In every season the dogwood is beautiful.

E

Canoes in the trees? It is a Cowichan story. Three hundred years ago there was a strong earthquake. It made a giant wave called a tsunami (tsoo-NA-mi). The wave smashed a village and tossed the canoes into the trees. Across the ocean, in Japan, people wrote about a tsunami from the same earthquake.

Every day BC has small earthquakes no one can feel. Scientists say another BIG ONE will come. No one can say when.

e

A tsunami hit Vancouver Island in 1964. This photo from a newspaper shows a boat that was tossed onto a street.

F

Years ago glaciers scoured deep mountain valleys. The valleys that ended at the ocean made **fjords**. Fjords are deep, long fingers of ocean with steep, rocky sides. In B.C., few roads reach the fjords. So if you want to see a fjord, you often have to travel by boat or plane.

BC has many fjords. In fact, if the wrinkled coastline stretched out straight, it would reach from Victoria to Halifax.

f

Photo: Adam Crysler

Climb The Chief for a great view of Howe Sound, one of BC's many fjords.

G

The Nisaqually people called them gwe-duk. That means digs deep. Now we write **geoduck** and say GOOey duck. And they are no kind of duck at all!

Geoduck is the biggest bivalve (an animal with two shells) that burrows. Geoducks live 60 cm (2 feet) deep in sand on BC's beaches.

This clam can grow as wide as a piece of writing paper. Its siphon (SI-fon), or neck, sticks out that far again. The siphon pokes up above the sand to eat small sea creatures.

The oldest one found was 146 years old.

g

A geoduck is not often on the sand because it can dig very fast.

Haida Gwaii (HI-da G'WHY) is a string of islands. The name means Islands of the People. The islands have been cut off from the coast for thousands of years. The Haida share their home with plants and animals that live only there.

In 2003 scientists found a unique slug no one had seen before. The scientists believe this slug has lived on Haida Gwaii through the ice ages. The glaciers did not reach the mountaintops where this slug still lives.

h

This slug is just one one of the wild creatures or plants found only on Haida Gwaii.

I

Scientists study glaciers to learn how the earth changes.

The **Illecillewaet** (Il-lu-SILL-oo-it) Glacier comes close to the railway in Rogers Pass. From the 1800s, people took pictures of the glacier. Scientists use the pictures to measure how much the glacier shrinks and grows. Then they can tell how much snow fell and how warm it was in the past.

Glaciers are not only important for science. When they melt, they give water to rivers. People visit glaciers to ski on them or to take pictures. They are also beautiful.

i

Photo: Professor Dan McCarthy, Brock University and Mas Matsushita, Parks Canada

1931

1887

1887

1906

1898

Sir Donald / Perley Rock Trail

Great Glacier Trail

The white lines on the photo show how much of the valley the Illecillewaet glacier filled at different times.

J

Jade is a symbol of BC. In nature it looks like any other dark rock. Hit nephrite (NEF-rite) jade with a carpenter's hammer. The jade won't break. That's because it is the world's toughest stone.

With the right tools, artists use jade to make beautiful carvings and jewelry.

In 2002 in the north of BC, people found the most valuable piece of jade ever. It is too big to fit in a pick-up truck. But when it is polished, the jade is pure enough to be a necklace—for a giant!

j

Polar Pride, the biggest piece of jade in the world, had to be cut apart to remove it from the mine.

K

There is a forest under the Pacific Ocean—the bull **kelp** forest. A tree on land has roots. A bull kelp plant has a holdfast instead. The holdfast grips onto rocks on the ocean floor and supports bulbs and long fronds that float on the top of the ocean. The bulbs and fronds protect the animals of the sea forest below. In winter, storms pull the holdfasts loose. The kelp floats to the beach. When strong waves toss kelp high onto shore it rots and becomes soil to feed the land forest.

k

Would you like to visit this forest under the Pacific Ocean? This one shelters fish from predators.

L

Not many people have seen a **lynx**. These timid wild cats live in the interior (middle) of BC. At night, big eyes help them hunt snowshoe hares, rodents, and birds. Long tufts of hair on their ears help them hear. Then they spread the toes of their big hairy feet to bound over the snow. In the day they hide quietly in thickets.

East of Fort Nelson, a mother lynx is leading her three cubs safely into the bush.

Marmots live in mountain meadows.

In winter, they hibernate in groups in burrows.

In summer, they come out to eat green plants. When one sees danger, it whistles to warn its friends. Then, they all dash back under the ground.

The town of Whistler is named for the warning sound.

BC has three kinds of marmot. The Vancouver Island marmot is almost extinct, but people are working to bring the number of marmots up. In 2003 there were only 30 wild Vancouver Island marmots. Now there are almost 200.

People working with the Marmot Recovery Foundation are helping the group of Vancouver Island marmots to continue to grow.

N

Cougar Brook growls through the land near Rogers Pass. Then it drops from sight. Underground, it dissolves the limestone rock.

There, the brook has made a maze of caves 6 km (3.7 miles) long. They are called the **Nakimu** (NAK-i-moo) caves.

In the caves, bacteria (bak-TEER-ee-a), limestone, and water combine to make moonmilk. The soft ooze covers the walls.

Nakimu has the most moonmilk of any place in the world.

The first white people who visited the caves touched the walls. The caves still hold those 100-year-old handprints.

n

The Nakimu Caves are protected. People can visit only on guided tours.

O

The copper in **octopus** blood makes the blood blue. But that isn't the only octopus colour. If an enemy comes near, an octopus squirts out dark ink. Then it swims away to hide. Its body changes colour to match the rocks and plants around it.

The giant Pacific octopus lives only four or five years. But it can weigh 270 kg (600 pounds)! That is big. Since it has no bones, it can slither into very small holes.

o

This scuba diver got a close-up look at a mid-sized giant Pacific octopus.

P

Some men wanted to build a newsprint mill. Mills needed to be near running water. The men chose the second shortest river in the world. **Powell River** was only 1 km ($^5/_8$ mile) long. But it made enough power so the mill owners could give the extra power to the town for free. People didn't turn off all their lights at night.

From the water, travelers could see Powell River in the night. So Powell River was called The White City.

The mill still makes paper. But now people turn off their lights.

p

Can you see the dam at the end of Powell Lake? The water falls from the dam to give power to the mill in the distance.

Q

Quesnel (kwu-NEL) Lake is the biggest lake in BC. It is also the seventh deepest lake in the world (530 m or about $\frac{1}{3}$ mile). The bottom of very deep lakes is a mystery. So scientists are studying **Quesnel Lake.**

For a long time, Quesnel Lake had very few salmon. Now it has more than one half of the salmon in the Fraser basin. Will the lake tell its secret?

q

Photo: Geoff Moore

This is only the North Arm of Quesnel Lake. It is 40 km (25 miles long). The East Arm is 55 km (34 miles) long, and the main lake is 80 km (50 miles) long.

R

Go as far south as you can in British Columbia. You will be on nine tiny islands called **Race Rocks.** No people live there.

The name comes from the strong racing tides. Many ships have crashed onto the rocks. Lighthouse keepers used to live there to warn ships. Now people only visit.

Cold Pacific Ocean currents stir up food for sea creatures. The food comes from deep down, up to the rocks. Fish, birds, sea lions, harbour seals, and elephant seals all come to this excellent seafood restaurant.

r

This photo is taken from the lighthouse. No one lives here all the time, but the keeper stays here when he has work to do on the island.

S

Salmon spawn (lay their eggs and fertilize them) in rives, lakes, or streams. Then they usually die. The young swim away. They live for years far from their first homes. Most salmon swim out in the ocean, sometimes 1600 km (1000 miles) away. But all salmon go back to their first home to spawn.

BC has five kinds of salmon. The spring salmon is the biggest. The heaviest one caught weighed 41.4 kg (93 pounds). The sockeye wins the salmon beauty contest.

S

Photo: Mark Kaarremaa

Many people love to watch the beautiful red of the sockeye salmon coming home to spawn.

Tree of Life. What a great name for BC's official tree! It can grow for up to 2000 years.

Even 100 years after it falls, the western redcedar's (red-SEE-darz) wood is still strong enough to make shingles.

Redcedar is beautiful. It smells good. It takes a long time to rot.

The first people used it to make dugout canoes, house planks, bentwood boxes, masks, paddles, and other tools. They used the inner bark to make rope, clothes, and baskets.

They also made medicine from this giant tree.

t

The western redcedar supports other life in the forest.

U

When the reindeer are dancing on the roof, it's because they are **ungulates**. Their hooves are really toes. So ungulates walk on their toes like dancers.

BC's reindeer are called caribou. Their hooves are big and round like snowshoes to help them walk on snow. Even a baby caribou one day old can run faster than a human.

Caribou can smell lichens growing deep under the snow. Then they use their hooves to dig for food.

u

This female caribou roams back and forth between British Columbia and Alberta in a national park. The only female ungulate with antlers is the caribou.

Vancouver Island is the biggest island on the west coast of North America. Prince Edward Island would fit into Vancouver Island more than 5 times.

On the west side of Vancouver Island, huge waves wash the shore where giant trees still stand tall. In the middle, tall mountains cut the island in half. On the east side, the island has the mildest climate in all of Canada.

If you visit Vancouver Island, you can see Henderson Lake, the wettest place in Canada, and Della Falls, Canada's tallest freefalling waterfall.

Della Falls is about seven times as tall as Niagara Falls, but has much less water.

A bird that climbs trees? That's the **woodpecker**. Short legs, strong, pointed toes, and springy tail feathers help the bird travel over tree trunks to build homes and find food.

Most woodpeckers poke their barbed tongues into holes to spear insects. The rare Williamson sapsucker drinks sap. The end of its tongue is like a brush. Like other sapsuckers, it leans back when it eats so it won't get its breast feathers sticky.

W

Photo: Diane Weismiller

This young Hairy Woodpecker enjoys treats hidden in a feeder by his photographer friend. He will lose the red mark on his head when he is an adult.

X

The **Xeni Gwet'in** (hu-NEE gwu-T'EEN) live in the valleys at the foot of the Snow Mountains in the Tsilhqot'in (chill-KOE-tin).

They value the old ways. They catch fish and smoke them. They gather mountain potatoes. They pick and dry berries. They dry meat that they hunt. They can eat these good things all winter. They also pick plants for tea and medicine.

The people look after a wild horse herd. They protect the horses' territory from logging and mining. They catch the horses and train them to use for packing and riding.

Families work together to get ready for winter. The bucket holds wild potatoes these people dug with the special tool the woman is holding.

The first people used **yew** wood to make bows, paddles, and other tools. They made medicine from the bark.

Deer, elk, moose, and caribou can eat yew. People can't. Most parts of the yew are poisonous to people.

It is also poisonous to cancer. Taxol from the bark of yew trees helps doctors fight cancer.

y

The bright yew berries last only a short time. Yew trees can be hard to find in the forest because they do not grow close together.

Z

Zinc is an amazing bluish-white metal. Carmakers use zinc to protect cars from rust. You can find zinc in bridges, fridges, rubber, coins, batteries, buildings, trumpets, and toys. It protects skin from the sun and helps to heal cuts.

For almost 100 years BC had the biggest zinc mine in the world in Kimberley. It is closed now. Deer and elk graze and people ski on the land that was once a mine. But there is still a big smelter nearby in Trail. The smelter takes zinc and other material from rock and makes it useful to people.

Z

Photo: Bruce Voyce

Bruce Voyce works on his galvanized eagle sculpture that watches over Central Park, Burnaby.

ABOUT THE BOOK

When the phrase, "amazing British Columbia" popped into my head, I thought, That's an alphabet book! In just a few minutes I had an alphabetical list of things that amazed me.

After six-and-a-half years of research, I've changed a few things on the list. I've also learned so much! I've met many wonderful people who shared information and photographs.

I couldn't put everything into the book, so I also built a Web site. It has the references I would have put into the back of the book, information about the photographers, and links to lots of other information about each entry so you can keep learning, too.

One difference between a Web site and a book is that the Web site can keep growing while the book will stay between two covers.

You can find out a lot more about this book, including more information about how I wrote it, by going to **AmazingBritishColumbia.com.** There will even be a place for you to add the amazing things you know about BC. I hope I'll meet you there.

Here I am after I'd driven for hours down a long dirt road in a heavy rain.

For more information on any of the subjects in this book go to AmazingBritishColumbia.com